The Magic of Making A DIFFERENCE

One CAN Make a Difference

Author: Dr. Marlena E. Uhrik

Illustrator: Aiden Huddleston

Gift Edition

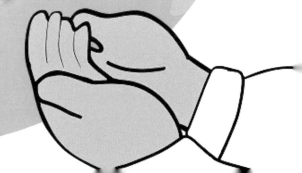

Archway Publishing books may be ordered through booksellers or by contacting:

Archway Publishing
1663 Liberty Drive
Bloomington, IN 47403
www.archwaypublishing.com
844-669-3957

Because of the dynamic nature of the Internet, any web addresses or links contained in this book may have changed since publication and may no longer be valid. The views expressed in this work are solely those of the author and do not necessarily reflect the views of the publisher, and the publisher hereby disclaims any responsibility for them.

Any people depicted in stock imagery provided by Getty Images are models, and such images are being used for illustrative purposes only.
Certain stock imagery © Getty Images.

ISBN: 978-1-6657-6938-9 (sc)
ISBN: 978-1-6657-6937-2 (hc)
ISBN: 978-1-6657-6936-5 (e)

Library of Congress Control Number: 2024925470

Print information available on the last page.

Archway Publishing rev. date: 12/05/2024

This book belongs to

_____

The Magic of Making A DIFFERENCE

One CAN Make a Difference

Written by Dr. Marlena E. Uhrik

Illustrated by Aiden Huddleston

Published by

ALL WAYS LEARNING, LLC

www.AllWaysLearning.org

Gift Edition

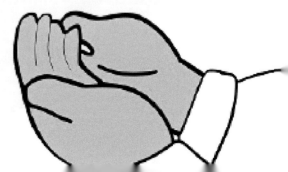

"The first time I heard Marlena tell this story, it brought tears to my eyes. I could really relate to the feelings and the many messages and lessons in the book. I am thrilled that this story is now written in a storybook form so that the message can be shared in a broader way with more people. This simple yet profound book provides the reader with a unique experience of hope, joy, and the realization that One CAN Make a Difference. At a time when there seems to be conflict, confusion, and the feeling of things going askew, the world needs this message now!"

– Alicia Price, CPCC, Certified Business and Life Coach

"This book is a great lesson for kids and a reminder for adults alike who want to make a bigger difference in the world. I highly recommend this to my mom friends and anyone with small children." – Katrina Sawa, Business Coach and 13x Int'l Best-Selling Author

Dedication

The Magic of Making a Difference: One CAN Make a Difference is dedicated to those young and old who dare to have dreams big and little.

Written to inspire and empower those who dream, and even those who have given up on their dreams, this true story is meant to share hope, inspiration, and realization of the magic that occurs when one says, "I can." Let this legend be the energy for embracing the true spirit of "One CAN Make a Difference."

"Marlena crafts a touching children's story that beautifully illustrates the importance of empathy, persistence, and small actions. The relatable characters and beautiful illustrations by Aiden bring the story to life, making it a heartwarming and insightful read for all ages. Through Lizzy's journey, children will gain a sense of empowerment and kindness. This book is a must-read, leaving a lasting impression on young minds." – River Easter, MA, Coach, Speaker, Author

The Story

It was a cold, wet, winter's day.
The sweet smell of cinnamon and hot oatmeal was coming from the kitchen. It made Lizzy hurry to get dressed for school while her brother was just starting to brush his teeth. On this particular day, Lizzy was very excited about something she wanted to share with her mom.

Lizzy went into the kitchen where her mom was busy fixing breakfast for the three of them. Lizzy did not know that her mom, a single parent, always seemed to struggle to put food on their table. Even though there was not much food to prepare, Lizzy's mom always managed to make things work for her family.

Lizzy ate quickly and took her bowl to the

kitchen sink.

"Mom," she said with excitement.

"Guess what? Our school is having a canned food

drive for hungry kids that don't have enough to eat,

and the class that collects the most canned goods

will win a pizza party." She just knew her third-

grade class could win!!!

Lizzy's mom looked at Lizzy's big eyes and said, "I am so sorry, Lizzy. We do not have enough food to share with others." Feeling super sad to hear her mom's words, Lizzy sighed, her teary eyes sank, and she left the room.

A few minutes later, everyone got into the car and was off to school. No one said a thing.

It seemed like a sad day, but Lizzy loved school. She was smart in lots of ways even though some things were hard for her to learn.

One of the things she loved best about school was seeing her friends there. Recess time was her favorite time because she got to play and run and talk with her friends.

When she was in the classroom, people called her the class clown because she always liked making people laugh---even though her teacher did not always approve.

It was the next day, and little Lizzy got ready for school as she always did. She still really wanted to bring some cans of food for the canned food drive. She wanted her class to win, but most importantly she wanted to bring something to help! She wanted to be part of her class helping others.

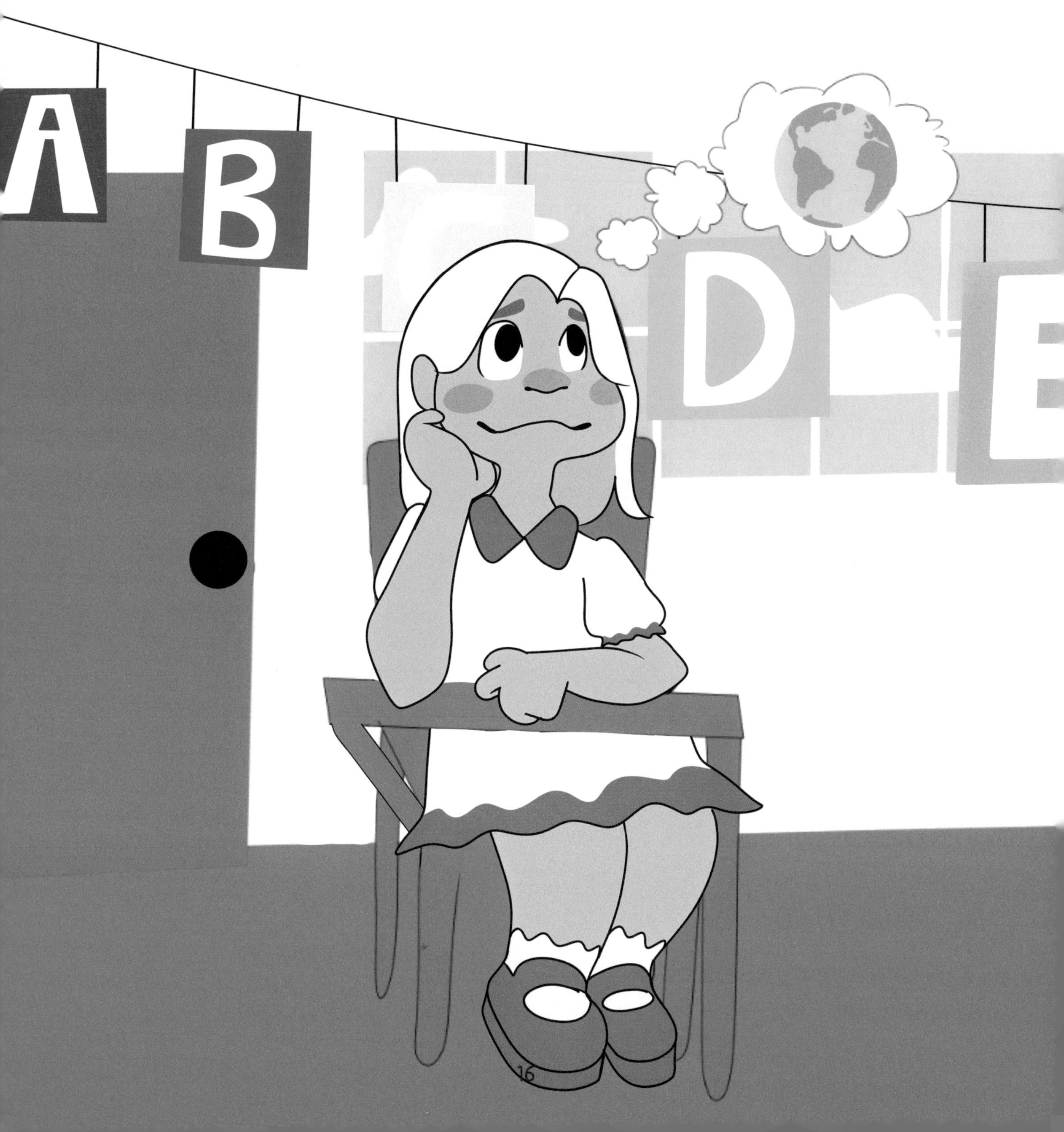
A
B
D
E

Lizzy decided she would ask her mom again. "Mom, can I PLEASE bring some canned foods to the canned food drive?" Her mom shook her head and sighed, and said again, "No. I am sorry, Lizzy." "We just do not have enough to share with others." Lizzy sighed and walked away. Even though she felt sad and disappointed, Lizzy was determined to find a way that she could make this work.

It was the last day of the canned food drive and Lizzy still had nothing to bring. Lizzy would not give up. That morning she ate her breakfast in silence and took her bowl to the kitchen sink like she always did. This time, with eyes so big and a heart so full, Lizzy looked at her mom and said, "Mom. Can I bring at least one can to the canned food drive?"

This time, her mom stopped and stood there. In that moment, Lizzy's mom could see, hear, and feel how much this really meant the world to her daughter. Before Lizzy knew it, her mom was looking and reaching as far back into the kitchen cupboard, as far as she could reach.

22

Then, to everybody's surprise, Lizzy's mom handed Lizzy a can of bamboo shoots. "Here. Here is a can of bamboo shoots.

I will not be using these bamboo shoots soon. Take this can to school for the canned food drive." Lizzy was thrilled beyond words! She had a can to take to the canned food drive.

24

A few days passed. The canned food drive was over, and the results were in. Lizzy came running home from school so excited. "Mom! Mom! Guess what? Our class won! Our class won the canned food drive... by one can!"

Lizzy's mom stood in the kitchen and hugged her daughter tightly. "I am so proud of you! You never gave up. You kept asking me and I kept thinking I did not have enough food to share." It was in that moment that Lizzy's mom was so grateful for what she had learned from Lizzy. With tears in their eyes and smiles on their faces, Lizzy and her mom understood, in a new way, that One CAN Make a Difference.

In that magical moment, Lizzy felt so happy knowing that she helped feed hungry kids and that she brought the one can that made a difference. Her mom got inspired too and started a movement to feed more families. Many people from all around joined in to help feed thousands and thousands of kids and families all because of One CAN.

Let us always remember that we each have the magic of making a difference no matter how big or little, young, or old.

One CAN, I Can, and We All Can

How CAN You Make a Difference Today?

How can YOU make a difference?

(Write your thoughts here.)

How will you FEEL when you make a difference? (Write your thoughts here.)

What are some of your DREAMS?

(Write your thoughts here.)

Draw a picture of someone who Makes a Difference in your life.

Unlock the Power of Positive
Impact with 52+ Ways Kids CAN
Make a Difference

www.AllWaysLearning.org/52ways

SCAN ME!

Sign up for our Facebook Page:
The Magic of Making a Difference

SCAN ME!

Post how you have made a difference.
Inspire others!
Let's continue making a difference together!

Special Thanks

Immense gratitude goes to my husband, Bill Wheelock, who has graciously supported the work that I do throughout our many years together. He has always demonstrated "cheerful cooperation" and a willingness to learn new technology to support the development and production of this awesome book along with so many other projects we have worked on together for the betterment of all.

Special thanks also to the amazing and gifted talent of our illustrator, Aiden Huddleston, who captured the essence and meaning of this story and conveyed that so beautifully. Special acknowledgment also goes to Aiden's family, especially his amazing mom, Vonetta Huddleston, for her tireless support and faith in this project.

Last, but not least, I am forever grateful to my daughter, Liz Grant, who taught us all the amazing lessons and demonstrations of believing in yourself, and your dreams, and never giving up.

One CAN, I Can, and We All Can Make a Difference!
Inspiration For This Book

Liz Grant is the author's daughter and the inspiration for this book. Liz is a professional comedian who has opened for Dana Carvey, Robin Williams and won the Brian Regan Impression Contest. Jim Harbaugh, former head coach of the SF 49ers, said she "made me laugh so hard my sides hurt". Liz lives in Northern California with three demented cats. Visit her at www. LizGrant.com.

About Our Amazing Illustrator
Aiden Huddleston

Hi, my name is Aiden Huddleston and my realization for the love of art began ever since I can remember. I love drawing, making cakes, and customizing characters. I love art because it is a way for me to express my creativity. This has been so fun to bring Dr. Marlena's vision to life. My parents, my two brothers, my sister, and my extended family have always been so encouraging! I appreciate the love and support from all of you! Thank you so much!! You can follow me on Instagram @created-by-aiden.

The Story Behind the Story
By Dr. Marlena E. Uhrik, Author

As a single Mom to my two kids, I often felt lost and alone. I questioned my worth and my place in the world. It was during this difficult time that my daughter's unwavering determination shattered my beliefs of doubt, lack, and inadequacy.

Who could forget that moment when she came home bursting with excitement as she shared the news that her class had won a canned food drive with just one can---the one can of bamboo shoots that she brought! It was the One CAN that made the difference!

In 1992, this spark evolved into a beacon of inspiration, compelling me to launch a grassroots movement against childhood hunger within my community. What initially seemed overwhelming was fueled by the memory that One CAN, and "I CAN " make a difference. My endeavor garnered attention, rallying volunteers from diverse sectors of the community to improve the lives of Hayward, California's youth and families. This momentum propelled me to be recognized as a Community Hero, an Olympic Torchbearer in 1996, and a notable presence in the United States Congressional Record.

From this, The Kids' Breakfast Club blossomed, changing thousands of lives. Let us spread this inspiration, reminding all of us of our potential. Our dreams can make waves, small gestures, or big impact. We hold the power to transform and inspire. Will you join this movement? One CAN, I CAN Make a Difference! Discover more at TheMagicofMakingaDifference.com.

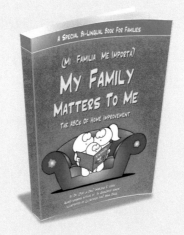

As you finish reading "The Magic of Making a Difference", you may find yourself inspired to take that first step toward creating your own ripple effect.

To help you turn inspiration into action, this book includes 12 Tip Sheets designed for families, schools, places of worship, clubs, and organizations. These resources are packed with information, practical ideas and activities to strengthen social-emotional learning skills, deepen understanding, and discover meaningful ways to make a difference.

Whether you're gathering with friends, teaching in a classroom, or organizing with your group, these Tip Sheets provide a roadmap to broaden your impact and create lasting change.

The tools and insights here can help you create an even bigger, better impact--whether your goal is to make your family stronger, your community more compassionate, or the world a better place. Let them be your guide as you turn the message of "The Magic of Making a Difference" into meaningful action. Now.

TIP SHEET #1

Howard Garder's Theory of Multiple Intelligences Based on Eight Intelligences

Many parents worry whether or not their child will be smart enough to "make the grade." So much emphasis is placed on homework, test scores and grades in school.

Below is a list of research that has been done by Howard Gardner who revolutionized the way educators think about intelligence. He recognizes that we are a combination of "intelligences" or learning styles that help us process, perform, and understand information. See if you can figure out how your child is smart!

IT'S NOT HOW SMART YOU ARE -- IT'S HOW ARE YOU SMART?

1. Linguistic children with this kind of intelligence enjoy writing, reading, telling stories or doing crossword puzzles.

2. Logical-Mathematical children with lots of logical intelligence are interested in patterns, categories and relationships. They are drawn to arithmetic problems, strategy games and experiments.

3. Bodily-Kinesthetic children process knowledge through bodily sensations. They are often athletic, dancers or good at crafts such as sewing or woodworking.

4. Spatial children think in images and pictures. They may be fascinated with mazes or jigsaw puzzles, or spend free time drawing, building with Legos or daydreaming.

5. Musical children are always singing or drumming to themselves. They are usually quite aware of sounds others may miss. These kids are often discriminating listeners.

6. Interpersonal children who are leaders among their peers, who are good at communicating and who seem to understand others' feelings and motives possess interpersonal intelligence.

7. Intrapersonal children may be shy. They are very aware of their own feelings and are self-motivated.

8. Naturalist children are more in tune with nature. They are interested in nurturing and exploring the environment.

A PLACE FOR YOUR NOTES
REFLECTION QUESTIONS

After reading the Tip Sheet, take a moment to reflect on what you've learned and how you can apply it in meaningful ways.

1. What stood out to you?
   • Identify the key takeaways or insights that resonated most with you.

_____

_____

_____

2. How will you put this knowledge into action?
   • Think about specific steps or strategies you can use to apply what you've learned in your daily life, with your family, or in your community.

_____

_____

_____

3. Who could benefit from this information?
   • Consider people, groups, or organizations you can share these ideas with to broaden their impact and inspire others.

_____

_____

_____

TIP SHEET #2

What Matters Most to Kids?

Here are some responses to a classroom assignment that I gave to my Kindergarten-1st grade class. You will notice that there is quite a range of things that are important to children 5-7 years old--everything from getting a new toy to world peace.

(The original wording is included. For privacy reasons, names have not been included.)

WHAT MATTERS MOST TO ME:

1. I wish for my 8th birthday.
2. I wish I can help Dr. Martin Luther King, Jr. and I can get a toy.
3. I wish my Mom well. I wish my cat fun.
4. I wish for a teddy bear.
5. I wish everyone was rich.
6. I wish the whole wide world to be friends.
7. I wish that I could go where ever I want to and do whatever I want.
8. I wish that everyone would not die.
9. I wish my Mom and my Dad love me and I wish I had friends.
10. I wish to get toys.
11. I wish my Grandmother had new pants.
12. I wish my Mom and my Dad wouldn't fight and everyone else.

A PLACE FOR YOUR NOTES
REFLECTION QUESTIONS

After reading the Tip Sheet, take a moment to reflect on what you've learned and how you can apply it in meaningful ways.

1. What stood out to you?
   • Identify the key takeaways or insights that resonated most with you.

_____

_____

_____

2. How will you put this knowledge into action?
   • Think about specific steps or strategies you can use to apply what you've learned in your daily life, with your family, or in your community.

_____

_____

_____

3. Who could benefit from this information?
   • Consider people, groups, or organizations you can share these ideas with to broaden their impact and inspire others.

_____

_____

_____

TIP SHEET #3

Having Family Fun in the Kitchen

Some of the most enjoyable times a family can have together are in the kitchen cooking up great things. Cooking together can be a special bonding time for everyone--a time for discovery, fun, and laughter.

This can be a special time for creating some of your favorite foods, and a great teaching time for math, science and physics. Simple math lessons can be learned about quantities of things (i.e. a teaspoon vs. a tablespoon--which one is bigger?), how things change shape (like popovers starting from a blob of flour to a puff pastry), and how heat or cold can change the properties of what you are working with like boiling or freezing water. It's also a great time to teach new vocabulary words, and new skills such a stirring, blending, and measuring. Cooking also teaches discipline, following instructions, and proper procedures for doing things. Remember though, safety first!

Learn from world-renowned celebrity Chef Alex Cheswick, the three ways you can create a fun, educational food experience with your kids. Listen as he shares with My Family Matters To Me, his experiences with his own daughter, Mia. The entire story of Alex's journey is also available at www.MyFamilyMattersToMe.com under the What's New tab. Please also visit Alex's website for some incredibly beautiful photos of food prepared by Alex along with some of his great insights. www.alexcheswick.com

Enjoy!

A PLACE FOR YOUR NOTES
REFLECTION QUESTIONS

After reading the Tip Sheet, take a moment to reflect on what you've learned and how you can apply it in meaningful ways.

1. What stood out to you?
   • Identify the key takeaways or insights that resonated most with you.

_____

_____

_____

2. How will you put this knowledge into action?
   • Think about specific steps or strategies you can use to apply what you've learned in your daily life, with your family, or in your community.

_____

_____

_____

3. Who could benefit from this information?
   • Consider people, groups, or organizations you can share these ideas with to broaden their impact and inspire others.

_____

_____

_____

TIP SHEET #4

Restorative Justice

How Does this Pertain to Parenting?

Restorative Justice, or RJ, as it is sometimes known, has proven to be a viable way of dealing with conflict and tension especially in the school settings. What is interesting about RJ is that it is not a program, but more of "a way of being." Suspensions at some schools using RJ have dropped by 51% since last year. Interwoven with RJ, is another approach to discipline that is called Positive Behavioral Interventions and Supports also known as PBIS.

Basically, these two strategies combined, have provided more self-discipline and have helped build the capacity for individuals to resolve conflicts. This combined system offers opportunities to focus on teaching the desired behaviors and looks at environmental issues as well. In other words, this is a "whole-child" approach based on developing intrinsic values. Often in a school setting, students, educators, and parents sit down with a mediator to talk about an incident and determine the appropriate response. A focus is on repairing harm. Students are held accountable for their actions, but also deal with the root cause of the conflict. (Sources include The Christian Science Monitor, March 31, 2013; The Washington Post, January 5, 2014.)

A lot can be said for applying some of these same principles to disciplining kids at home or in a classroom. Building self-responsibility, empathy, and understanding are key factors in helping our children become responsible students/citizens. There is much more "buy-in" when:

1. A system of accountability is well defined

2. Rules are made together as much as possible

3. Consequences for breaking the rules are determined together

4. There is an intention to see and understand the inter-connected nature of all things

How can you apply some of these principles to your own parenting skills?

A PLACE FOR YOUR NOTES
REFLECTION QUESTIONS

After reading the Tip Sheet, take a moment to reflect on what you've learned and how you can apply it in meaningful ways.

1. What stood out to you?
   • Identify the key takeaways or insights that resonated most with you.

_____

_____

_____

2. How will you put this knowledge into action?
   • Think about specific steps or strategies you can use to apply what you've learned in your daily life, with your family, or in your community.

_____

_____

_____

3. Who could benefit from this information?
   • Consider people, groups, or organizations you can share these ideas with to broaden their impact and inspire others.

_____

_____

_____

TIP SHEET #5

Mindfulness for Moms

The practice of mindfulness is slowly but surely making an appearance in a variety of settings such as many of the nation's hospital systems, churches, schools, Attention Deficient Disorder (ADD) clinics, yoga practices, and even prisons.

Scientific research indicates that mindfulness meditation may reduce stress-related illness, boost long-term health of the body's cells, and enhance one's sense of well-being. It has also been found to contribute to pain relief alertness, memory, and cognitive performance. Mindfulness meditation can also help people deal with anger management, anxiety, and depression. "It's not like snapping your fingers and you're there," said Bernard, teacher from Davis. "It's like learning a musical instrument. It takes time and commitment and discipline." (Sacramento Bee, April 1, 2013)

Mindfulness starts with a commitment to want a calmer, more peaceful you. This can work for busy parents who are often overwhelmed with an avalanche of family activities and responsibilities. With mindfulness practices, people report greater freedom from stress and worry. Look in your copy of My Family Matters To Me and find the letter "B" for Belly Breathing. You will find a simple exercise for you and your family to do together (or alone). Enjoy the all-around benefits of mindfulness by focusing on your breathing and an awareness of being in the moment. There are a variety of additional resources to be found on the internet.

How could five minutes of mindfulness help you cope with everyday living? How can you make that happen?

A PLACE FOR YOUR NOTES
REFLECTION QUESTIONS

After reading the Tip Sheet, take a moment to reflect on what you've learned and how you can apply it in meaningful ways.

1. What stood out to you?
   • Identify the key takeaways or insights that resonated most with you.

_____

_____

_____

2. How will you put this knowledge into action?
   • Think about specific steps or strategies you can use to apply what you've learned in your daily life, with your family, or in your community.

_____

_____

_____

3. Who could benefit from this information?
   • Consider people, groups, or organizations you can share these ideas with to broaden their impact and inspire others.

_____

_____

_____

TIP SHEET #6

I Love You, Daddy

I love the plaque my sister and I gave our Dad on Father's Day several years ago. It says, "Anyone can be a father, only some can be a Dad." This plaque still hangs proudly in his den where this 87 year old man sits quietly during the day.

It wasn't always like that. I had gone through my own rebellious time, making my parents wrong for almost everything in my life. Now that I am older, I wonder why we have to go through such a tumultuous time when we just can't seem to find it within us to really appreciate our parents. Maybe it's not until we become older or become parents ourselves that we even come close to understanding what our parents went through to put together a life for us.

I distinctly remember that one Father's Day when I called my Dad. There I was on the phone, standing in the kitchen, looking out onto my backyard. I was just going to wish him a Happy Father's Day and give him the usual report on the weather and say that everything was fine. Something happened during that call---I'm not sure what---and all of a sudden I realized that the words, "I love you, Daddy" came out of my mouth. I don't remember what made me tell him that. I just remember the long silence on the other end of the phone and the soft sound of his tears. You see, I had not told my Dad those three words for a very long time. All I know is that it surprised me and I know it really surprised him.

Now that I am 64 years old, I've gotten a lot smarter and a lot more thankful for the man I still call Daddy. I cherish the time we spend together, listening to those same old stories and hearing him laugh. I look into those eyes and see years of pain and joy and wisdom. I make sure I tell him I love him every time we talk and I wonder how many days I have left to say, "I love you, Daddy."

Do you have a Dad or someone who is like a Dad to you to say, "I Love You"?

A PLACE FOR YOUR NOTES
REFLECTION QUESTIONS

After reading the Tip Sheet, take a moment to reflect on what you've learned and how you can apply it in meaningful ways.

1. What stood out to you?
   • Identify the key takeaways or insights that resonated most with you.

_____

_____

_____

2. How will you put this knowledge into action?
   • Think about specific steps or strategies you can use to apply what you've learned in your daily life, with your family, or in your community.

_____

_____

_____

3. Who could benefit from this information?
   • Consider people, groups, or organizations you can share these ideas with to broaden their impact and inspire others.

_____

_____

_____

TIP SHEET #7
Summer Learning Loss

Kids can hardly wait for summer to get here. They are thinking about all of the free time they are going to have so that they can hang out with friends, watch TV, and basically kick back. The truth is that after about the third day of summer vacation, it is not unusual to hear, "I'm bored" or "There's nothing to do." The scary part is what research is showing about "Summer Learning Loss."

Here are a few facts:

1. Over summer break, students lose between one and three months worth of math and reading skills they learned during the academic year, an education professor at Duke University found.

2. Summer learning loss can account for two-thirds of the three grade level achievement gap between high-income and low-income students, Time reported.

3. By not being in a classroom for an extended period of time, summer break may dull the intellect of students who are not being academically stimulated, according to California's Department of Education.

So what's a parent to do?

Here are a few tips--most of them no or low cost:

1. Create an educational environment in your home.

2. Let your child choose books from the library that interest him/her.

3. Have plenty of basic art supplies--paper, felt pens, crayons, paste, stickers, and play dough to name a few.

4. Plan a picnic or excursion to local attractions. Check with your local Parks and Recreation Department.

5. Find educational apps or programs that will challenge and reinforce skills and knowledge.

6. Limit screen time.

7. Team up with a neighbor or friend and plan things together.

8. Take time to play outdoors.

If your child is in childcare, ask your provider what types of educational activities are planned for your child. What kind of learning experiences do you want your child to have?

A PLACE FOR YOUR NOTES
REFLECTION QUESTIONS

After reading the Tip Sheet, take a moment to reflect on what you've learned and how you can apply it in meaningful ways.

1. What stood out to you?
   • Identify the key takeaways or insights that resonated most with you.

_____

_____

_____

2. How will you put this knowledge into action?
   • Think about specific steps or strategies you can use to apply what you've learned in your daily life, with your family, or in your community.

_____

_____

_____

3. Who could benefit from this information?
   • Consider people, groups, or organizations you can share these ideas with to broaden their impact and inspire others.

_____

_____

_____

TIP SHEET #8

Camping in the Great Outdoors

Camping outdoors can be one of the finest family experiences ever. It is an opportunity to be together and have fun in new and exciting ways. Listed below are some notes from a friend, Mark Trail, an experienced camper:

1. Buy a book on the type of camping you are doing (car camping, backpacking, RV camping, etc.). Many such books are available on Amazon for under $5.00 used but in good condition! Google the "10 Essentials of Camping."

2. Have a "Plan B" for the technological devices taken for granted in the modern world like GPS or cell phones. A map and compass (and knowing how to use them) is a good example of having a Plan B.

3. Create a menu before you leave and buy all of the ingredients. Small stores in or around campgrounds can be extremely expensive. Chopping and mixing the ingredients ahead of time can save a lot of time and ice chest space while cooking outdoors.

4. Keep your food stored where critters like raccoons and bears can't get to it, such as in the trunk of a car. Note: hanging food in a sack from a tree limb doesn't often work very well--critters will still try to get to the food.

5. Be sure to have a good sleeping bag. Make sure that you insulate yourself from the ground in your tent/sleeping quarters.

6. Keep sanitary. Hand wipes and waterless antibacterial soap help greatly!

7. Campfires are good fun if you are in a safe place to have them (get a fire permit if camping in the wilderness). Don't forget to bring an axe to make kindling for your fire.

8. Children love campfires almost as much as they love roasting mouthwatering marshmallows and hot dogs!

9. Bring friends for the kids (and yourself) and you'll never run out of interesting games to play and topics to discuss. Bring books, board games, and other family fun activities for the youngsters and yourself.

10. Above all, be safe and have fun! Leave the modern world behind.

A PLACE FOR YOUR NOTES
REFLECTION QUESTIONS

After reading the Tip Sheet, take a moment to reflect on what you've learned and how you can apply it in meaningful ways.

1. What stood out to you?
   • Identify the key takeaways or insights that resonated most with you.

_____

_____

_____

2. How will you put this knowledge into action?
   • Think about specific steps or strategies you can use to apply what you've learned in your daily life, with your family, or in your community.

_____

_____

_____

3. Who could benefit from this information?
   • Consider people, groups, or organizations you can share these ideas with to broaden their impact and inspire others.

_____

_____

_____

TIP SHEET #9

Our Children as Citizens of the World

It occurred to me several years ago when I was back in the classroom teaching, that I had a more awesome responsibility than I had originally thought. I realized that I was preparing those little children with big eyes and bigger dreams, how to be citizens of the world. I began to see them as not only our future, but as our future leaders. What if we approached raising our children as though we are raising future leaders of the world? What skills would they need? How can we prepare them for things unknown?

What Are 21st-Century Skills?

Learning to collaborate with others and connect through technology are essential skills in a knowledge-based economy.

ATC21S started with a group of more than 250 researchers across 60 institutions worldwide who categorized 21st-century skills internationally into four broad categories:

1. Ways of thinking. Creativity, critical thinking, problem-solving, decision-making and learning

2. Ways of working. Communication and collaboration

3. Tools for working. Information and communications technology (ICT) and information literacy

4. Skills for living in the world. Citizenship, life and career, and personal and social responsibility

How are you teaching 21st Century skills to your child?

A PLACE FOR YOUR NOTES
REFLECTION QUESTIONS

After reading the Tip Sheet, take a moment to reflect on what you've learned and how you can apply it in meaningful ways.

1. What stood out to you?
   • Identify the key takeaways or insights that resonated most with you.

_____

_____

_____

2. How will you put this knowledge into action?
   • Think about specific steps or strategies you can use to apply what you've learned in your daily life, with your family, or in your community.

_____

_____

_____

3. Who could benefit from this information?
   • Consider people, groups, or organizations you can share these ideas with to broaden their impact and inspire others.

_____

_____

_____

TIP SHEET #10

Research Shows Your Child Will Succeed if...

All of the parents that I have taught and interviewed over the last 45 years have said the same thing--they want their children to succeed and have a better life than they had. While we as parents/caregivers provide the basics such as food, clothing and shelter, research shows that three (3) things can help determine whether or not children and young people succeed:

Meaningful Relationships--Meaningful relationships help children and young people attain the psychological and social skills that are essential for success in education and in life. These relationships can be formed with their parents and family members, with their friends and peers, and with staff members in their schools, extra curricular activities, and programs. Caring adults in their neighborhoods and communities can also play a meaningful role in the lives of children, young people, and their families.

Meaningful Work/Sense of Contribution--Children are more successful when they feel valued, supported, and cared for by the adults in their school and community. We need to offer children and young people meaningful opportunities to participate in the classroom, in our schools, and community.

Expect the Best--It is important that as parents and educators we have high expectations that all children and youth can succeed by doing their best--no matter what they might try. Students will work to reach the highest academic levels when they know that adults listen to them, believe in them, and expect their best.

Provide opportunities for children and their families to experience more communication and connectedness. This time together can build more meaningful relationships, and help discover, reinforce, and appreciate a sense of individual uniqueness in each and every family.

A PLACE FOR YOUR NOTES
REFLECTION QUESTIONS

After reading the Tip Sheet, take a moment to reflect on what you've learned and how you can apply it in meaningful ways.

1. What stood out to you?
   • Identify the key takeaways or insights that resonated most with you.

_____

_____

_____

2. How will you put this knowledge into action?
   • Think about specific steps or strategies you can use to apply what you've learned in your daily life, with your family, or in your community.

_____

_____

_____

3. Who could benefit from this information?
   • Consider people, groups, or organizations you can share these ideas with to broaden their impact and inspire others.

_____

_____

_____

TIP SHEET #11

Oh Great! Here Come the Holidays!

On July 25, 2014 my husband announced to me, "Only 5 months until Christmas!" Immediately, I could feel my shoulders go up around my ears and my breathing stop for a moment! Yipes! I realized I was already stressed out just thinking about Christmas coming in 5 months!!! I had to ask myself, "What am I going to do differently so I do not get so stressed out just thinking about the holidays?"

So how can we enjoy the holidays? Is it possible to create those wonderful Norman Rockwell moments when people seem to like each other and be content? Or could that we part of the problem??? Do we have realistic expectations??? Something to think about...

Let's take a look at three things I am going to do differently to help reduce my stress around the holidays:

1. Decide the kind of experience I want to have with my friends and family for the holidays. Quiet, formal dinner? Potluck? Games and activities? Conversation? Music? Special holiday movies?

2. Get organized ahead of time to support less stress. Use a calendar, journal, and a To Do list. Look to see what I can do way ahead of time, like buy stamps for those Christmas cards in July. (?!) Shop for gifts way before the holiday rush to avoid the crowds and traffic. Schedule some "down" time.

3. Keep It Simple Sweetheart (KISS). Remember what is important to me--celebrating the importance of family. Express my appreciation and gratitude for my friends and family.

What three things can you do differently that will help reduce your stress and create the holiday experiences you want to have?

63

A PLACE FOR YOUR NOTES
REFLECTION QUESTIONS

After reading the Tip Sheet, take a moment to reflect on what you've learned and how you can apply it in meaningful ways.

1. What stood out to you?
   • Identify the key takeaways or insights that resonated most with you.

_____

_____

_____

2. How will you put this knowledge into action?
   • Think about specific steps or strategies you can use to apply what you've learned in your daily life, with your family, or in your community.

_____

_____

_____

3. Who could benefit from this information?
   • Consider people, groups, or organizations you can share these ideas with to broaden their impact and inspire others.

_____

_____

_____

TIP SHEET #12

Don't Tell Me the Sky is the Limit When There are Footprints on the Moon!

Inspiring Your Genius Child

We have often heard the expression, "The Sky is the Limit." What's unique about the quote, "Don't Tell Me the Sky is the Limit When There are Footprints on the Moon!" is that it expands our thinking as to what is possible. It's this kind of thinking that can provide the motivation and empowerment for doing things bigger than we thought we could. As parents, we have the unique opportunity to provide this kind of motivation for our children.

What happens when we view our kids from a place of recognition of their strengths, possibilities, and support? With a positive attitude, there are many ways that parents can provide the inspiration and motivation for their children. Imagine how it would be if all children were recognized for being a genius with their own unique gifts and talents?

We hope you have found some valuable tips in our Tip Sheets. We feel strongly that one of the best gifts a parent can give their children is to keep learning about how to be an even better parent. It has often been said that children do not come with an instruction manual and guess what? They don't! And it's not easy being a parent! With that said, there are many resources now available to help us keep informed.

To inspire you and your genius child, here is what we have shared in the previous Tip Sheets. Parents learned more about recognizing that their children have multiple intelligences; and that things that matter most to children are the relationships with people in their lives; that simple experiences such as time shared together in the kitchen can bring fun, laughter, and learning; that there is a difference between discipline and punishment; that we need to take time for ourselves and prepare for the day; that parents/grandparents need to be recognized and honored for who they are to the family; that children need to be intellectually stimulated even when school is not in session; that new, shared experiences are valuable times together for bonding; that our job as parents is to prepare our children to be citizens of the world; that children will succeed with three important qualities; that children get stressed out too, and that we can help by managing our own stress; so that with love, care, skills, knowledge, and education, we have children ready to take on the world and leave their footprints on the moon. Happy Landing!

A PLACE FOR YOUR NOTES
REFLECTION QUESTIONS

After reading the Tip Sheet, take a moment to reflect on what you've learned and how you can apply it in meaningful ways.

1. What stood out to you?
   • Identify the key takeaways or insights that resonated most with you.

_____

_____

_____

2. How will you put this knowledge into action?
   • Think about specific steps or strategies you can use to apply what you've learned in your daily life, with your family, or in your community.

_____

_____

_____

3. Who could benefit from this information?
   • Consider people, groups, or organizations you can share these ideas with to broaden their impact and inspire others.

_____

_____

_____